PUMPKINS!

By Natalie Whitney

Illustrated by Nancy Gibson Nash

Houghton Mifflin Company Boston

Atlanta Dallas Geneva, Illinois Palo Alto Princeton

Here's a pumpkin seed.

It grows in the ground.

3

It grows to be a vine.

4

Soon the vine grows flowers.

The flowers become pumpkins.

Pumpkins are good in pies

Or as Jack-o'-Lanterns!